D0982084

THE
Little Book
— OF —
CELTIC
WISDOM

THE

Little Book

— OF —

CELTIC
WISDOM

Compiled by

GIULIETTA WOOD

ELEMENT

Shaftesbury, Dorset ❖ Rockport, Massachusetts
Brisbane, Queensland

© ELEMENT BOOKS LIMITED 1997

Published in Great Britain in 1997 by
ELEMENT BOOKS LIMITED
Shaftesbury, Dorset SP7 9BP

Published in the USA in 1997 by
ELEMENT, INC
PO Box 830, Rockport, MA 01966

Published in Australia in 1997 by
ELEMENT BOOKS LIMITED
for JACARANDA WILEY LIMITED
33 Park Road, Milton, Brisbane 4064

*Cover illustration: MS 58 fol. 202v
Trinity College Library, Dublin*

Designed by
BRIDGEWATER BOOKS

Printed and bound in Italy by Imago
British Library Cataloguing in Publication data available
Library of Congress Cataloging in Publication data available

ISBN 1 86204 049 4

*The publishers would like to thank the following for the use of pictures:
The National Library of Wales*

FOREWORD

CELTIC CULTURE has a reputation for poetic sentiment and mystic wisdom. Although that reputation has been much enhanced by the romantic revivals of past decades, both Celtic verse and Celtic prose have the capacity to convey powerful universal sentiments through images drawn from the natural world, the codes of heroic behavior and a rich mythology. It has been said that the half-said thing was dearest to the Celts. This is clearly expressed in the characteristic mixture of nature poetry and proverbial wisdom. However, this observation on the nature of Celtic literature is perhaps best illustrated in narratives with their tantalising links between concrete action and symbolic image. Although we may never be certain about the exact meaning of these images in their original context, to a modern reader with modern sensibilities, they can be thought provoking and inspiring.

The contemporary descendants of the Celts, the
Irish, Manx and Scots-Gaelic speakers, the Bretons,
Welsh and Cornish have been marked
and influenced by very individual histories. As a
result there are many kinds of Celtic wisdom
literature and the differences are as important as the
similarities. The following selections reflect this
range and invite you to appreciate the diversity of
Celtic wisdom.

Who creature did first make Alpha?
Which is the fairest form of praise which
  the Lord made?
What food what beverage?
From what came his clothing
Who faced denial?
The might of a country's deceit
Why is stone hard?
Why is thorn sharp-pointed?
Who is hard as stone and salty as salt?
Why is the nose like a ridge?
Why is the wheel round?
Why does the tongue declare more
Than any organ?

Hanes Taliesin
16th century

hie pce duoy uwx de ui

Old is man when he is born
and young, young ever after.

Book of Taliesin

As the sigh of Uther for
the love of Ygraine,
the fair and splendid
And the sigh of Kynor for the
love of the beauteous
daughter of Urien
Such is the sigh of the bard for
the lovely object of his affection.

Bardic Triad

The knight came to the place where Arthur and Owain were seated at chess. And they perceived that he was harassed and vexed and weary as he came towards them. And the youth saluted Arthur, and told him that the Ravens of Owain were slaying his young men and attendents. And Arthur looked at Owain and said, 'Forbid thy Ravens'. 'Lord,' answered Owain, 'play thy game.' And they played. And the knight returned back toward the strife, and the Ravens were not forbidden anymore than before.

The Dream of Rhonabwy

For 'tis one of their tenets
That nothing perisheth, but
(as the Sun and year) everie thing
goes in a circle, lesser or Greater,
and is renewed and refreshed in
its revolutions.'

The Secret Common-wealth
17th century

O Lord give thy blessing
And in blessing, strength
And in strength, understanding
And in understanding, knowledge
And in knowledge, knowledge
of righteousness
And in knowledge of righteousness,
love for it
and in loving it, love for all creation
And in all creation, the love of god
God and all goodness.

Iolo Morganwg's Bardic Invocation

At last Oisin said to his wife: 'I wish I could be in Erin to-day to see my father and his men.'

'If you go', said his wife, 'and set foot in the land of Erin, you'll never come back here to me…

It is three hundred years,' said she, 'since you came to this kingdom with me. If you must go to Erin, I'll give you this white steed to carry you; but if you come down from the steed or touch the soil of Erin with your foot, the steed will come back that minute and you'll be where he left you, a poor old man.'

'I'll come back never fear…', said Oisin. 'But I must see my father and my son and my friends in Erin once more: I must have even one look at them.

Oisin in Tir na n'Og

Three things that constitute a physician
A complete cure, leaving no blemish
behind, a painless examination

Irish Triad

He who seizes the wolf's mane
without a spear in his hand
Should always keep a brave heart
beneath his cloak.

The Gododdin

Near Glasfryn Lake is a well called Ffynnon Grassi. In olden times it was a fairy well. Grassi's duty was to keep the well covered. One evening she forgot, and the water gushed out. At last it overwhelmed one of the fairies' dancing rings, and they stopped the overflow, but not before Glasfryn Lake had been formed. Grassi, overcome with remorse, walked to and fro; wringing her hands and weeping. The fairies changed her into a swan. In this form she haunted the lake for many years, after which time the fairies allowed her to resume her human shape. There is still to be seen, on certain nights of the year, a lady wandering up and down the high ground, weeping and wailing. If she is not Grassi who is she?

W. Jenkyn Thomas

A country without language
is a country without a heart.

Traditional Welsh saying

Don't see what you see
Don't hear what you hear
Don't tell what you know
of Cough a na Looba.

Irish rhyme against the Fairies

'Dallwaran Dallbenn's sow, that came burrowing as far as the Headland of Penwedic in Kernyw and then took to the sea…

At Maes Gweith in Gwent she dropped three grains of wheat and three bees, and ever since Gwent has the best wheat and bees.

From Gwent she proceeded to
Dyfed and dropped a grain of barley
and a porker, and ever since Dyfed
has the best barley and pigs…

Afterwards she proceeded to Arfon
and in Lleyn she dropped the grain
of rye, and ever since Lleyn and
Eifionydd have the best rye…'

The Triad of the Sow

The corn is in the haggard and
  all made right
You will not know which reaper
  was first or last.

Manx proverb

Guess what is upon thee,
and thou dost not feel it on thee,
It isn't thy bones, it isn't thy hair,
  and it isn't thy locks.
Answer: A man's name.

Manx riddle

ñ debet ab hoſtio rece[
nem brachiū ſui cū uge[

lede n longitudio

usus ianitorem.

di

o
au
r
pu
ro

ei

ar

co

de

fu

Paramours' love, like the flowing tide
Wanderers' love, like wind off a sea rock
Married men's love, like a ship sailing to
harbour.

Gaelic saying

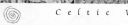

A green hill far from me,
Bare bare when I reach it.

Manx proverb

There was shown them a wonderful island, and in it a great grove of marvellous beauty laden with apples…A sparkling rivulet of wine flowed through the midst of the grove; and where the wind blew through the trees, sweeter than any music was the rustling it made. The O'Corras ate some of the apples and drank from the rivulet of wine and were immediately satisfied. And from that time forth they were never troubled by either wounds or sickness.

The Voyage of the O'Corras

 25

Elphin's customary chief bard am I
My original country is the land of
the Cherubim
John the Magician called me Merlin
But now all kings call me Taliesin.
I received inspiration from the cauldron
of Ceridwen
I was among the harp poets to
Leon Lychlyn
I was with Gwynfryn in the court
of Cynfelyn
In stock and fetters a day and a year

I was revealed in the land of the Trinity
And I was prophet through the
entire universe
And I shall be until Doomsday on
the face of the earth
And no one knows what my flesh is
whether meat or fish
I was almost nine months in the womb
of Ceridwen the witch
I was formerly Gwion Bach
but Taliesin am I now.

Hanes Taliesin
16th century

Like a blind man's progress through a hedge
Or walking on rough rocky slopes
Like the baying of a hound in an empty glen
Is learning to the ignorant.

Gaelic saying

Like an otter at a river mouth
Like a falcon to a bird of the moor
Like a dog to a cat
Like a cat to a mouse
Is the son's wife to her mother-in-law.

Gaelic saying

Choicest Delights – A love of pure intent for a maiden, white as chalk, beautiful and gentle, graceful and stately.

Longing for the lady fair and noble, consumes me night and day.

Ariethiau Pros
16th century

Three things which inspire the poet:
  An eye to see the world clearly
  A heart which feels sincerely
  And courage to render faithfully.

Bardic Triad

Three things that are forever cold:
  A greyhound's nose, a gash on a stone
  And the hearth of a miser's son.

Welsh proverb

The three functions of speech:
  To recite, to argue, to tell a story.

Bardic saying

What is man, compared with this, but haze
And smoke and fog and grass and shame
A brittle glass, a scent and roses
A trembling reed, and wind and foam

Cofiwch Angau

Your little book is not lost,
It is in the sea eighteen fathoms deep,
In the mouth of a fish who is guarding it.
Only three pages are ruined,
One with water, one with blood
And one with the tears of my eyes.

Breton ballad

Alas, how wretched through great complaint
  comes the prophecy to the line of Troy,
A coiling serpent proud, without mercy, with
  golden wings from Germania.
It shall conquer Lloegr and Prydein, from the
shore of Scandinavia to the Severn

Then shall the Britons be like prisoners,
  aliens in status to the Saxons
Their Lord they shall praise
Their language they shall preserve
Their land they shall lose, except Wild Wales,
Until comes a certain time after long penance
When the two proud people will be equal.
Then will Britain receive its land and its crown
  and foreign people will disappear
And the words of the angel of peace and war
Will be secure about Britain

Hanes Taliesin
16th century

...iauter... ...Iosepl'...uatum...
ciarii camerie: est domus portarii.

Et cecisin debet hie ancu...
yn in hospicio suo. s. tres...
dysos plenos osbarne. et ta comme...

mayk & altam medietate ky
Si filiu ul' filia ñ huit ? toc
ciam ei rex habeat excepto.
morte. De auib; & demdi

jquis nidu accipit abst
rer reddat. vel ulna Mhr

The end of every ship her drowning
The end of every kiln its burning
The end of a lord his dispraising
The end of health is a sigh.

Gaelic saying

What is the best thing
man can have?
A life that's even,
just and brave.

Welsh proverb

The loch is no heavier for carrying
the wild duck
The horse is no heavier for the bridle
The sheep is no heavier for its wool
And the body is no heavier for its
intelligence.

Gaelic saying

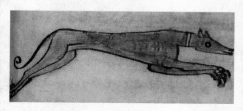

In the evening by the fire my father flows
    back to me.
The things we did together, and myself often
Unkind. His kindly courtesy ghosts
Its way here and shelters my heart under its
    proud and simple wing.

When the great emptiness swelled him
    beyond the void,
I did not realise he would remain within me
    despite a departure so final.
And that he would dart into my head as though
    relaxing at home
In the evening by the fire with his feet on
    the shelf of my mind.

Behind the world's back, in the evening
    by the fire

His love wanders down. Behold it comes back.
It infuses my veins to create their power
To shine on my memory of the days that were
    so dear.
And I too will wander along the evening of
    some day
To the hearth where all is bound together,
    the store of all beloved things.

BOBI JONES
In The Evening

Idleness is the sword's praise
And rust its honour

Welsh Englyn

Bendegeidvran came to land, and the fleet with him by the bank of the river. 'Lord,' said his chieftains, 'Knowest thou the nature of this river, that nothing can go across it, and there is no bridge over it? What,' said they 'is thy counsel concerning a bridge?' 'There is none' said he 'except that he who will be chief, let him be a bridge. I will be so' said he. And then was that saying first uttered, and it is still used as a proverb. And when he laid down across the river, hurdles were placed upon him, and the host pased over thereby.

The Four Branches of the Mabinogi

There is no knoll nor mound
Nor grassy golden hillock
That sometimes is not happy
sometimes dark and fearful.

Gaelic saying

'O Cormac, grandson of Conn,'
said Carbery,
'What is the sweetest thing you have heard?'
'Not hard to tell,' said Cormac.
'The shout of triumph after victory.
Praise after wages.
A lady's invitation to her pillow.'

The Instructions of King Cormac

Three times a hound's age,
the age of a horse
Three times the age of a horse,
the age of a man
Three times a man's age,
the age of a deer
Three times the age of a deer,
the age of an eagle
Three times the age of an eagle,
the age of an oak.

Gaelic saying

He who comes late on a Saturday
And leaves early on Monday
For all the help I'll get from him
I'd rather he stayed away.

Gaelic saying

This teaches how to distinguish between truth and falsehood and exemplifies a phrase without contention if it is dark.

This teaches how to know present and future events and fortunes, both good and bad. And whosoever is versed in this will know, as he goes his way, what may befall him. And were he to see two armies fighting he would knew before the battle which would prevail; and from this art the emperors of Rome knew how their men were faring to the ends of the earth if they were on an errand.

Dialectics and Astrology
from the Seven Liberal Arts
16th century

ACKNOWLEDGEMENTS

While every effort has been made to secure permissions to
reproduce copyright material, if there are any errors or
oversights regarding copyright material, the publishers
apologise and will make suitable acknowledgement in any
future edition. All translations unless otherwise stated are my
own. I would like to express my thanks to Professor Bobi Jones
for his kindness is allowing me to translate his poem, to
Dr John MacInnes and to Professor B.F. Roberts for their
translations. I would also like to thank the University of Wales
Press, CMCS Publications and the Folklore Society for
permission to reproduce or adapt material.

pp. 7, 26, 32: *Hanes Taliesin* from Elis Gruffudd's Chronicle.
p. 8: *The Book of Taliesin*
pp. 8, 11: *The Secret Common-wealth*, Robert Kirk, The
Folklore Society 1976.
p. 9: Bardic Triad from Charlotte Guest's edition of *The
Mabinogion*.
p. 10: From *The Dream of Rhonabwy*, in Charlotte Guest's
translation of *The Mabinogion*.
p. 12: Iolo Morganwg's invocation for the Gorsedd ceremonies
which open the Eisteddfod in Wales.
p. 14: From *The Goddodin*.

p. 14: 'The Triads of Ireland', from *Selections of Ancient Irish Poetry* translated by Kuno Meyer. P. 15: 'Grace's Well' from *The Welsh Fairy Book*, W. Jenkyn Thomas, University of Wales Press, 1995.

p. 16: 'The Green Isles of the Ocean' from *The Welsh Fairy Book*, W. Jenkyn Thomas, University of Wales Press, 1995.

p. 17: Traditional Welsh saying.

p. 17: From *Myths and Folktales of Ireland*, collected by Jeremiah Curtin in 19th century.

p. 17: John Rhŷs translation of Welsh Triad from *Celtic Folklore, Welsh and Manx*.

p. 17: From *Fairy Legends and Traditions of the South of Ireland* collected by T. Crofton Croker.

p. 20: William Cashen, *Manx Folk-lore*.

pp. 21, 25: 'The Voyage of the O'Corras', from P.W. Joyce, *Old Celtic Romances*.

pp. 24, 30: From *Welsh Proverbs with English Translations*, Henry Halford Vaughan 1889. New translation by J. Wood.

p. 25: A.W. Moore, *The Folk-Lore of the Isle of Man*.

pp. 28, 37, 36, 39, 42, 43: Traditional Gaelic saying, translated by John MacInnes.

p. 29: From *Dafydd Maelienydd's Choicest Delights*, translated by B.F. Roberts.

p. 31: *Cofiwch Angau* (Memento Mori), by Y Ficar Pritchard.

p. 31: 'Gwerz Skolan', from *Breton Ballads,* Mary-Ann Constantine, CMCS Publications, Aberystwyth, 1996.

p. 38: *In The Evening,* by Bobi Jones.

p. 40: Welsh Englyn, quoted on war memorials in West Wales.

p. 41: From *Branwen Daughter of Llyr,* in Charlotte Guest's translation of *The Mabinogion.*

p. 42: 'The Instructions of King Cormac', from *Selections of Ancient Irish Poetry* translated by Kuno Meyer.